A SOUTHERN
Night Before
CHRISTMAS

Written by Kelly Kazek

Illustrated by Michelle Hazelwood Hyde

Visit us at **southernthing.com**

Printed in Canada
First edition October 2020
ISBN: 978-1-57571-992-4 (hardback)

'Twas the night
before Christmas and all
through the house

We were sticky and sweaty
'cause this is the South,

Mom wanted to host a
traditional Yule

So she turned on the air
so we could stay cool.

Our stockings hung neatly all in a row
The logs on the fireplace were mostly for show,
Our sleeping bags lined the floor by the dozens
Since there weren't enough beds to fit all the cousins.

The fridge was stocked with platters and bowls

And ten covered dishes held ten casseroles,

Six kinds of cakes met our eager eyes

Then MeeMaw walked in with two pecan pies.

Aunt Ruth was giving each cousin a kiss
As the children compared their Christmas wish lists,
The twins asked for games, Sue wanted a kitten
Ted wanted whatever Randy was gettin'.

Emma wanted a doll
and Sutton some candy

Ted hoped for
a trampoline for his
cousin Randy,

No snowsuits or
sleds or any cold-weather
present

The winters 'round
here were always quite
pleasant.

Mom left some biscuits
and a glass of sweet tea
In case Santa needed a
real Southern treat,

She added ice cubes and a couple of straws

Then all was ready for old Santa Claus.

Then a sudden loud noise had the household abuzz
And we all ran downstairs to see what it was,

We knew when we heard a clip-clopping hoof
Santa's sleigh and his reindeer were up on the roof.

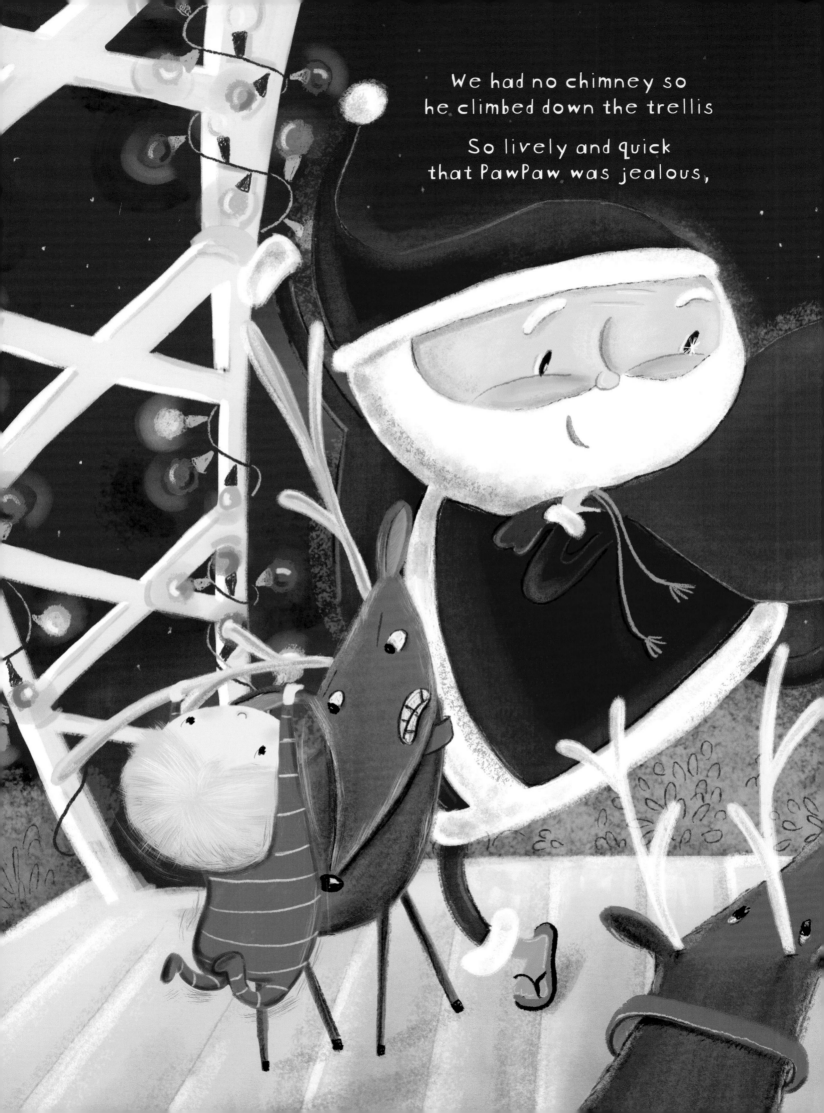

He was dressed as
expected in his red suit

But on his feet he wore
flip flops instead of his boots.

Santa came in the house and
set down his sack

Then picked up a biscuit for
a much-deserved snack,

He unloaded the gifts
between sips of sweet tea

And arranged them quite
neatly under the tree.

"There are games for the twins,
a kitten for Sue,

"A doll and some candy and a trampoline, too,

"Gifts for each cousin," Santa
said with a drawl,

"Hope you like them," he winked,
"Merry Christmas, y'all."

As he tossed his red sack over his shoulder
He saw Becky Leigh, and said lightly to scold her,
"Back to bed, little one. You've got to be smart
"Young'uns need sleep, bless your sweet little heart."

As he readied to go, he saw
Becky Leigh ponder,

"Is it true," she asked Santa,
"that you're from up yonder,

"From up in the North where
they don't say 'y'all'

"Where people talk funny and
not with a drawl?"

Santa laughed and his tummy
sloshed with sweet tea

"I go north to cool off,"
Santa told Becky Leigh,

"But don't worry," he said,
patting her head

"I love the South.
Now off to bed."

Before we could utter,
"You're welcome to stay"

Santa was suddenly back
in his sleigh,

As he flew overhead,
he exclaimed in delight:

"Blessed Christmas to y'all
and to y'all a good night!"